Dreams Unleashed

A Blueprint for Achieving Your Ultimate Potential

DREAMS UNLEASHED

First edition. January 3, 2024.

ISBN: 979-8224208937

Written by Maurice Philippe.

Table of Contents

Maurice Philippe

❖ Introduction

Dreams are the silent whispers of the soul, guiding us towards our true potential. In this chapter, we embark on a journey to unravel the profound meaning of dreams—those personal aspirations and goals that ignite the fire within and propel us toward the extraordinary. Let us delve into the significance of pursuing dreams and explore the transformative power they hold.

A: Definition of Dreams

In the quiet recesses of the human soul, dreams emerge as the silent architects of our destinies. They are the whispered promises we make to ourselves—a tapestry of personal aspirations and goals that weave the narrative of our lives. As we embark on this exploration of dreams, let us unfurl the meaning behind these ethereal desires and understand how they shape the very fabric of our existence.

1. Personal Aspirations and Goals

Our journey begins with an introspective gaze into the depths of our desires. Dreams are not just the ephemeral musings of an idle mind; they are the blueprints of our potential, outlining the grand architectures of our aspirations. They embody the spectrum of our yearnings, from the modest to the monumental, creating a symphony of purpose that resonates within us.

Consider the artist who dreams of capturing the sublime on canvas or the entrepreneur whose aspirations soar to create transformative technologies. These personal dreams are the threads that embroider the canvas of our lives, crafting a narrative uniquely ours. They give us direction, infuse our daily pursuits with meaning, and serve as beacons guiding us through the labyrinth of existence.

As we navigate the landscape of our own aspirations, we discover the kaleidoscope of dreams—ranging from the pursuit of knowledge and career success to the quest for meaningful relationships and personal growth. Each dream, no matter how humble or audacious, holds the potential to transform our lives.

2. Importance of Pursuing Dreams

Why do we embark on the pursuit of dreams with unwavering determination? The answer lies in the profound importance of this quest. Dreams are not frivolous fantasies; they are the heartbeat of a purpose-driven life. By pursuing our dreams, we engage in a profound act of self-discovery, uncovering hidden facets of our identity and unlocking the reservoirs of our potential.

Consider the athlete who dreams of standing on the podium, the scholar whose aspirations extend to unraveling the mysteries of the universe, or the humanitarian whose dream is to create positive change in the world. These dreams become catalysts for action, propelling us forward even when faced with challenges. They fuel our resilience, nurture our creativity, and transform obstacles into stepping stones.

The importance of pursuing dreams transcends individual fulfillment; it reverberates through the collective tapestry of humanity. The symphony of human achievement is composed of the harmonious pursuit of countless dreams—each note contributing to the rich melody of progress, innovation, and shared aspiration.

B: The Power of Dreams

In the vast expanse of human experience, dreams wield an extraordinary influence—a force that transcends the boundaries of the tangible and delves into the realm of inspiration and transformation. As we navigate the profound landscapes of dreams, we explore the motivational stories of individuals who have harnessed this power to achieve remarkable feats. Additionally, we delve into the scientific and psychological perspectives that shed light on the impact of dreams on our lives.

1. Motivational Stories of Individuals Who Achieved Their Dreams

The annals of history are adorned with narratives of individuals who dared to dream boldly, surmounting adversity to carve their names into the tapestry of human achievement. These stories are not mere chronicles of success but testimonials to the indomitable spirit that resides within every dreamer.

We traverse the pages of time to encounter figures like Marie Curie, whose dream of unraveling the secrets of the atom led to groundbreaking discoveries, and Steve Jobs, who envisioned a world where technology seamlessly melds with creativity. Their journeys are not just sagas of triumph but blueprints for those who aspire to turn their dreams into reality.

As we immerse ourselves in these tales, patterns emerge—patterns of perseverance, resilience, and an unyielding belief in the transformative power of dreams. Whether in the realm of science, arts, or entrepreneurship, these dreamers exemplify the extraordinary feats achievable when one listens to the whispers of their aspirations.

2. Scientific and Psychological Perspectives on the Impact of Dreams

Beyond the realm of inspiration lies the intricate interplay between dreams and the human psyche. What happens when we dream, and how do these subconscious adventures influence our waking lives? The marriage of science and psychology unravels the mysteries, offering profound insights into the tangible impact of dreams.

Neuroscientific exploration delves into the intricacies of the brain, revealing the physiological responses to dreams. Psychology, on the other hand, unveils the emotional and cognitive dimensions, showcasing how dreams serve as motivational engines that drive behavior and shape our perceptions of self and the world.

Together, these perspectives form a mosaic that highlights the symbiotic relationship between dreams and human potential. By understanding the science behind our dreams, we gain a deeper appreciation for the innate power they possess to propel us toward our goals.

Chapter (1) Understanding Your Dreams

In the labyrinth of dreams, the second chapter unfolds—a guide to understanding the intricacies of our aspirations. Here, we delve into the art of identifying passion and setting clear goals, crucial steps on the journey toward realizing the full potential of our dreams.

A: Identifying Your Passion

In the kaleidoscope of dreams, the quest for fulfillment begins with the discovery of passion—an intimate connection to the beating heart of our aspirations. This chapter serves as a guide, leading us through the profound process of identifying our passions. Through self-reflection exercises and the exploration of hidden desires, we unveil the raw essence of what makes our souls come alive.

1. Self-Reflection Exercises

At the core of identifying passion lies the art of self-reflection. In the hustle of daily life, amidst the myriad responsibilities and obligations, it's easy to lose sight of our authentic desires. This section introduces a series of self-reflection exercises designed to peel back the layers and reveal the core elements that define our passions.

Questions beckon us to contemplate our values, interests, and the activities that stir genuine joy. What brings a sense of fulfillment? When do we feel most aligned with our true selves? By engaging in these exercises, we embark on a journey of self-discovery, creating a roadmap that illuminates the path to our deepest passions.

2. Uncovering Hidden Passions

Passions, like undiscovered gems, often lie hidden beneath the surface, waiting to be unearthed. This section encourages exploration and experimentation as we seek to uncover these hidden desires. Through activities that transcend the ordinary, we venture into the realm of the unknown, acknowledging that our true passions may evolve and transform.

Revisiting childhood interests, trying new hobbies, and embracing novel experiences become gateways to uncovering hidden passions. The chapter emphasizes that the journey of self-discovery is an ongoing adventure, where each revelation adds nuance to the canvas of our dreams.

As we navigate the terrain of our own passions, we come to understand that identifying these desires is not a static process but a dynamic and evolving one. The whispers of our authentic selves become clearer, guiding us toward a profound understanding of the dreams that resonate at the core of our being.

B: Setting Clear Goals

Having unveiled the tapestry of our passions, the journey toward actualizing our dreams continues with the pivotal step of setting clear goals. In this chapter, we explore the art of translating aspirations into actionable objectives, employing the SMART goal-setting methodology, and understanding the delicate balance between long-term visions and short-term milestones.

1. SMART Goal-Setting Methodology

The path from passion to achievement is paved with well-defined goals. The SMART goal-setting methodology becomes our compass, guiding us through the process of crafting objectives that are Specific, Measurable, Achievable, Relevant, and Time-bound.

This section delves into the practical application of SMART criteria, illustrating how specificity provides clarity, measurability gauges progress, achievability maintains motivation, relevance aligns with our passions, and time-bound deadlines instill a sense of urgency. Through real-world examples and hands-on exercises, we learn to articulate our dreams in a manner that transforms them from abstract ideals into tangible, achievable goals.

2. Long-Term vs. Short-Term Goals

Dreams unfold across the tapestry of time, and effective goal-setting requires a harmonious blend of both long-term visions and short-term objectives. This section explores the nuanced relationship between these temporal dimensions, offering insights into the strategic balance required for sustained progress.

Long-term goals serve as beacons, providing direction and purpose for our overarching aspirations. Simultaneously, short-term goals become the stepping stones that maintain momentum and celebrate incremental victories along the way. By understanding and embracing the symbiotic nature of these goals, we navigate the ebb and flow of progress, ensuring that our journey is both purposeful and rewarding.

Through the process of setting clear goals, we empower ourselves to turn the abstract into the concrete, bridging the gap between passion and achievement. As we stand at the intersection of dreams and objectives, the chapters ahead beckon us to navigate challenges, create a roadmap to success, and cultivate the support systems that will sustain us on this transformative journey.

Chapter (2) Overcoming Obstacles

In the pursuit of dreams, obstacles stand as formidable challenges, testing the resilience of our aspirations. This chapter serves as a guide to navigate the common hurdles that often loom on the path to success. Through understanding the nature of challenges, and implementing strategies to overcome them, we fortify ourselves against the headwinds of adversity.

A: Common Challenges

In the grand tapestry of pursuing dreams, challenges emerge as shadows that test the resolve of even the most passionate dreamers. This chapter is dedicated to dissecting the common challenges that often stand as barriers between us and the realization of our aspirations.

1. Fear of Failure

At the crossroads of ambition and uncertainty lies the pervasive fear of failure. This section explores the roots of this fear and its profound impact on our journey. Through introspection and understanding, we navigate the paralyzing grip of failure anxiety and reframe it as a natural part of the growth process.

Real-life stories of individuals who faced and conquered the fear of failure become guiding lights, illuminating the transformative potential that lies within setbacks. The chapter invites us to embrace failure not as a stumbling block but as a catalyst for learning, resilience, and eventual success.

2. Lack of Resources

Resource scarcity, whether financial, informational, or otherwise, can cast a daunting shadow on our dreams. In this section, we delve into the dynamics of resource limitations, exploring how they manifest and impact our pursuits. By shifting our mindset from scarcity to resourcefulness, we uncover strategies to overcome constraints and foster creativity.

Through practical examples and case studies, we witness how individuals have navigated the challenging terrain of limited resources to carve out success. The chapter instills the belief that ingenuity and determination can be powerful allies in transforming scarcity into an opportunity for innovation.

As we dissect these common challenges, we lay the foundation for the next section—strategies to overcome these hurdles. The goal is not just to acknowledge the existence of challenges but to empower ourselves with the tools and mindset needed to surmount them.

B: Strategies for Overcoming Challenges

In the labyrinth of pursuing dreams, challenges are inevitable, but so too are the strategies to overcome them. This chapter is a guide to navigating the obstacles that stand between us and our aspirations. Through the exploration of building resilience and seeking support and mentorship, we equip ourselves with the tools to conquer adversity.

1. Building Resilience

Resilience is the bedrock upon which dreams weather the storms of adversity. In this section, we delve into the art of building resilience, an indispensable skill for navigating the unpredictable journey toward our goals. Through practical strategies and insights, we learn to bounce back from setbacks with newfound strength.

Cultivating a growth mindset becomes a focal point, encouraging us to view challenges not as insurmountable roadblocks but as opportunities for personal and professional development. The chapter explores the power of positive thinking, adaptive coping mechanisms, and the importance of self-care in fortifying our emotional and mental well-being.

Real-world examples of individuals who have triumphed over adversity through resilience serve as beacons of inspiration. By adopting these practices, we pave the way for not only overcoming challenges but emerging stronger and more resilient on the other side.

2. Seeking Support and Mentorship

No dream is realized in isolation, and seeking support is a fundamental strategy for navigating challenges. This section illuminates the importance of cultivating a robust support system, whether through friends, family, or mentors. By tapping into the wisdom and guidance of those who have traversed similar paths, we gain invaluable insights and perspective.

The chapter provides practical guidance on building effective support networks, emphasizing the reciprocity inherent in collaborative relationships. Mentorship emerges as a powerful catalyst for personal and professional growth, and we explore how the mentor-mentee dynamic can become a cornerstone in overcoming challenges.

Real-life stories of individuals who have found strength and solace through support and mentorship underscore the transformative power of collective wisdom. As we navigate the landscape of challenges, we discover that the shared burden is lighter and the journey more rewarding when undertaken with the encouragement and guidance of others.

Chapter (3) Creating a Roadmap to Success

In the journey toward the fulfillment of our dreams, the creation of a strategic roadmap is the compass that guides us through the twists and turns. This chapter unfolds the art of planning, organization, and adaptation to change—a roadmap that ensures we stay on course despite the challenges that may arise.

A: Planning and Organization

In the grand tapestry of turning dreams into reality, the art of planning and organization emerges as a compass, guiding us through the intricate pathways of achievement. This chapter is dedicated to the meticulous process of crafting a step-by-step plan and mastering time management techniques—key elements that transform aspirations into actionable goals.

1. Developing a Step-by-Step Plan

The journey toward success begins with a well-crafted plan—a roadmap that transforms lofty dreams into manageable, actionable steps. In this section, we delve into the intricacies of developing a step-by-step plan, breaking down ambitious goals into tangible tasks. Through practical insights and real-world examples, we learn the importance of granularity and specificity in planning.

Templates and exercises guide us through the process, offering a structured approach to articulate our dreams in a way that is both strategic and achievable. By dissecting overarching goals into manageable components, we gain clarity and direction, laying the foundation for a purposeful and systematic journey toward success.

2. Time Management Techniques

Time, the currency of achievement, demands a disciplined and strategic approach. This section explores time management techniques tailored to the pursuit of dreams. From prioritization methods to effective scheduling, we learn to optimize our time to maximize productivity and progress.

Real-world applications and case studies underscore the impact of efficient time management on the realization of our goals. The chapter aims to instill the discipline needed to balance competing priorities, ensuring that our time is an investment in the fulfillment of our dreams.

As we navigate the landscape of planning and organization, the chapters ahead beckon us to adapt to change, learn from setbacks, and celebrate milestones. Join me in this exploration of the transformative power of strategic planning—a cornerstone in the architecture of success.

B: Adapting to Change

In the dynamic journey of pursuing our dreams, change is the only constant. This chapter is dedicated to understanding the art of adapting to change—an essential skill that ensures our dreams remain resilient in the face of evolving circumstances.

1. Embracing Flexibility

Change is not an obstacle but an intrinsic part of the path to success. In this section, we explore the importance of embracing flexibility as a fundamental mindset. We delve into the resilience that comes from adapting to unexpected shifts and evolving circumstances, recognizing that the ability to pivot is a strength, not a weakness.

Real-life stories of individuals who have navigated change with grace become beacons of inspiration. The chapter encourages us to view flexibility not as a compromise but as a strategic advantage, allowing us to respond to the ever-changing landscape of our dreams with agility and purpose.

2. Learning from Setbacks

Setbacks, though challenging, are opportunities for growth and refinement. This section transforms setbacks from roadblocks into stepping stones. By adopting a mindset of continuous learning, we explore how setbacks provide valuable lessons that shape our strategies and strengthen our resolve.

Real-life stories of individuals who have turned setbacks into opportunities for growth serve as inspiration. The chapter emphasizes the importance of resilience and adaptability in the face of adversity, teaching us that setbacks are not the end of the road but rather detours on the way to success.

As we delve into the realm of adapting to change, we recognize that flexibility and the ability to learn from setbacks are not just survival skills but the very essence of thriving in the pursuit of our dreams. Join me as we embrace the transformative power of adaptability, paving the way for the chapters ahead—learning from setbacks, celebrating milestones, and ultimately realizing the full potential of our aspirations.

Chapter (4) Building a Support System

In the vast landscape of dreams, the journey becomes more meaningful when shared. This chapter delves into the art of building a robust support system—an essential foundation that nurtures aspirations, provides guidance, and amplifies the transformative power of dreams.

A: Family and Friends

In the symphony of dreams, the influence of family and friends resonates as a powerful and harmonious melody. This chapter delves into the profound significance of building a supportive foundation within our closest circles—those whose encouragement and understanding become the pillars upon which our aspirations can soar.

1. Nurturing Positive Relationships

Within the embrace of family and friends, we find a sanctuary where dreams are nurtured and strengthened. This section explores the importance of cultivating positive relationships with those who share in our journey. By fostering an environment of support and encouragement, we lay the groundwork for the flourishing of our aspirations.

Practical insights guide us in navigating the dynamics of familial and friendly relationships. The chapter emphasizes the reciprocity inherent in positive connections, illustrating how the strength of our dreams is magnified when rooted in the soil of genuine, uplifting bonds.

2. Communicating Dreams to Loved Ones

Effective communication becomes the bridge that spans the gap between individual dreams and collective understanding. This section delves into the art of articulating our aspirations to family and friends. Through clarity, passion, and openness, we not only secure the support of those dearest to us but also create a shared sense of purpose.

Real-life examples highlight the transformative impact of honest and open communication within families and friendships. The chapter empowers us to convey our vision authentically, fostering an environment where everyone feels invested in and contributes to the journey toward our dreams.

As we navigate the intricate dance of relationships within our inner circles, we recognize that the support of family and friends is not just a source of strength but a cornerstone in the edifice of our dreams.

B: Networking and Mentorship

In the expansive landscape of dreams, the power of connections extends beyond the immediate circle of family and friends. This chapter unfolds the transformative impact of networking and mentorship—key elements that enrich our journey, foster growth, and amplify the collective resonance of our aspirations.

1. Connecting with Like-Minded Individuals

Beyond our immediate circles lies a world of like-minded individuals whose shared passions can amplify the pursuit of our dreams. This section explores the significance of expanding our network, creating connections with those who resonate with our aspirations. Through collaboration, inspiration, and shared experiences, we cultivate a community that becomes a source of motivation and encouragement.

Practical strategies guide us in finding and building connections with individuals who share similar dreams. The chapter illustrates the power of a collective journey, showcasing how a network of like-minded individuals can contribute to the richness of our personal and professional growth.

2. Finding Mentors in Your Field

Mentorship, a guiding force, provides wisdom and perspective as we navigate the intricate paths toward our goals. This section delves into the transformative influence of mentorship, offering insights on finding mentors within our respective fields. By tapping into the knowledge of those who have walked similar paths, we accelerate our growth, gaining invaluable guidance and support.

Real-life mentorship stories become beacons of inspiration, highlighting the profound impact mentors can have on the trajectory of dreams. The chapter provides practical guidance on identifying, approaching, and cultivating relationships with mentors, emphasizing the reciprocal benefits inherent in mentor-mentee dynamics.

As we explore the realms of networking and mentorship, we recognize that the support system extends beyond our immediate circles, encompassing a broader community of collaborators and mentors. Join me as we continue to unravel the layers of collaborative growth, celebrating milestones, and realizing the full potential of our dreams.

Chapter (5) Cultivating a Growth Mindset

In the fertile soil of a growth mindset, dreams take root, flourish, and reach toward the sunlit heights of their full potential. This chapter explores the transformative power of cultivating a mindset focused on growth—a mindset that embraces continuous learning, values education and skill development, and harnesses the force of positive thinking to overcome self-doubt.

A: Embracing Continuous Learning

Within the dynamic landscape of dreams, the capacity for continuous learning serves as a compass, guiding us through uncharted territories of knowledge and skill development. This chapter is a voyage into the transformative power of embracing a mindset steeped in perpetual learning—a mindset that recognizes the importance of education, values skill development, and thrives on curiosity and open-minded exploration.

1. The Importance of Education and Skill Development

Education is the cornerstone upon which the architecture of our dreams is built. In this section, we delve into the profound significance of continuous learning as an ongoing and integral part of our journey. By understanding the symbiotic relationship between education, skill development, and the pursuit of our goals, we equip ourselves with the tools necessary to navigate the ever-evolving landscape of our aspirations.

Practical insights illuminate the dynamic interplay between education and skill development, providing guidance on how to integrate learning into the fabric of our daily lives. The chapter emphasizes that each new piece of knowledge acquired and every skill honed is a building block, fortifying the foundation upon which our dreams stand.

2. Staying Curious and Open-Minded

Curiosity is the spark that ignites the flame of lifelong learning. This section explores the importance of staying curious and open-minded as pillars of a growth mindset. By fostering a mindset that embraces curiosity, challenges become opportunities for discovery, and obstacles transform into gateways to innovation.

Practical tips and exercises encourage the development of a curious and open mindset, creating an environment where learning is not a task but a continuous and enriching experience. The chapter highlights that an open mind is a receptive canvas, ready to absorb the vibrant hues of new ideas and perspectives that propel us forward on our journey.

B: Positive Thinking

In the realm of dreams, positive thinking acts as the catalyst that propels aspirations from the realm of possibility to the shores of reality. This chapter unfolds the transformative power of cultivating a positive mindset—a mindset that incorporates affirmations, visualization techniques, and strategies to overcome self-doubt.

1. Affirmations and Visualization Techniques

Affirmations and visualization serve as the brushstrokes that paint the canvas of our aspirations with hues of positivity. This section delves into the art of crafting affirmations and incorporating visualization techniques as potent tools for cultivating a positive mindset. By intentionally shaping our thoughts and beliefs, we lay the groundwork for a mental environment that nurtures the pursuit of our dreams.

Practical guidance on the creation of affirmations and the incorporation of visualization into daily practices becomes a roadmap for infusing positivity into our mindset. The chapter illuminates how these techniques serve as powerful allies, reinforcing our belief in the feasibility of our dreams and fostering a sense of empowerment.

2. Overcoming Self-Doubt

Self-doubt, a shadow that often looms on the path to dreams, is confronted with resilience and determination in this section. By understanding the roots of self-doubt and implementing strategies to overcome it, we fortify the foundation of our growth mindset. The chapter guides us in reframing negative thoughts, building self-confidence, and embracing a mindset that views challenges as opportunities for learning and improvement.

Real-life stories of individuals who have triumphed over self-doubt become beacons of inspiration. The chapter underscores that a growth mindset not only acknowledges the existence of self-doubt but transforms it into a stepping stone for personal and professional development.

Chapter (6) Celebrating Milestones

In the journey towards our dreams, milestones are the markers that not only measure progress but also serve as opportunities for reflection, growth, and resilience. This chapter unfolds the importance of celebrating milestones—a practice that involves acknowledging achievements, reflecting on progress, rewarding oneself for accomplishments, and understanding the profound lessons that failures can impart.

A: Acknowledging Achievements

In the symphony of pursuing dreams, acknowledging achievements is the melody that resonates with the sweet notes of progress, dedication, and resilience. This section explores the profound importance of reflecting on progress and rewarding oneself for accomplishments—a practice that not only celebrates the journey but also fuels the spirit for what lies ahead.

1. Reflecting on Progress

The journey toward our dreams is a tapestry woven with moments of growth and triumph. This section delves into the significance of reflecting on progress as a means of acknowledging achievements. By taking intentional pauses to appreciate milestones, we gain a panoramic view of the path traversed, fostering a sense of gratitude and motivation.

Practical exercises guide us in cultivating a reflective mindset, allowing us to recognize and celebrate the incremental victories that contribute to the overall narrative of our aspirations. The chapter emphasizes that reflection is not just a celebration but a strategic pause—a moment to recalibrate, appreciate the journey, and draw inspiration for the road ahead.

2. Rewarding Oneself for Accomplishments

Rewards are the jewels that adorn the crown of our accomplishments, infusing joy into the journey and affirming our dedication. This section explores the art of rewarding oneself for achievements. By intentionally creating a system of personal rewards, we reinforce the connection between effort and celebration, nurturing a positive feedback loop that sustains our momentum.

Practical strategies guide us in designing personalized reward systems that align with our aspirations. The chapter illuminates how the act of rewarding oneself becomes a potent motivator, turning each achievement into a moment of celebration and self-appreciation.

B: Learning from Failures

In the mosaic of dreams, failures are not dead ends but rather dynamic stepping stones to growth and success. This section illuminates the transformative power of learning from setbacks—a practice that elevates failures from mere stumbling blocks to invaluable sources of knowledge and resilience.

1. Extracting Lessons from Setbacks

Setbacks are not signs of defeat but rather arrows pointing us towards crucial lessons. This section explores the art of extracting lessons from setbacks, transforming failures into stepping stones to success. By dissecting the root causes and outcomes of setbacks, we uncover insights that fortify our resilience and inform future strategies.

Real-life examples illustrate how setbacks can become catalysts for growth when approached with a mindset of continuous learning. The chapter underscores that acknowledging and understanding failures are integral components of the journey toward our dreams.

2. Using Failures as Stepping Stones to Success

Failures, when viewed through the lens of a growth mindset, become invaluable stepping stones towards success. This section guides us in embracing failures not as roadblocks but as opportunities for refinement and innovation. By channeling the lessons learned from setbacks, we recalibrate our strategies, enhancing our chances of success in subsequent endeavors.

Inspiring stories of individuals who have transformed failures into launching pads become beacons of resilience. The chapter emphasizes that the most successful journeys are often paved with the stones of setbacks, each failure propelling us closer to the realization of our ultimate potential.

Chapter (7) Sustaining Success

As we stand atop the peaks of achievement, the journey doesn't conclude but transforms into a narrative of sustaining success. This chapter delves into the delicate balance required to nurture a flourishing life amid accomplishments. It explores the art of avoiding burnout, prioritizing self-care, and giving back—elements crucial to the continued success of our endeavors.

A: Balancing Work and Life

In the ongoing saga of success, the delicate dance of balancing work and life emerges as an art form, requiring mindfulness, resilience, and a commitment to well-being. This section navigates the intricacies of avoiding burnout and prioritizing self-care—a pivotal aspect of sustaining success in the pursuit of our dreams.

1. Avoiding Burnout

The pursuit of success, while exhilarating, can sometimes lead us perilously close to burnout. This section explores the signs of burnout and provides strategies to avoid its detrimental effects. By recognizing the importance of maintaining a healthy equilibrium between ambition and well-being, we fortify ourselves for the sustained journey ahead.

Practical tips and exercises guide us in implementing preventive measures against burnout. The chapter underscores that avoiding burnout is not just a matter of physical health but a strategic imperative for long-term success—a conscious decision to cultivate a sustainable and fulfilling lifestyle.

2. Prioritizing Self-Care

Amid the demands of success, self-care becomes the compass that steers us toward holistic well-being. This section delves into the significance of prioritizing self-care as a non-negotiable component of sustaining success. By adopting practices that nourish the mind, body, and soul, we establish a resilient foundation for the continued pursuit of our dreams.

Practical strategies and self-care rituals become the keystones of a thriving life. The chapter emphasizes that self-care is not an indulgence but a necessity—a deliberate choice to safeguard our physical and mental health as we navigate the intricate tapestry of work and life.

B: Giving Back

As we stand on the summits of our achievements, the echoes of success gain their fullest resonance when we extend a hand to uplift others. This section explores the transformative power of giving back—a multifaceted endeavor that involves mentoring others and contributing to the community. In the symphony of sustained success, giving back becomes the harmonious chord that resonates beyond individual accomplishments.

1. Mentoring Others

The torch of success shines brightest when passed on to illuminate the paths of others. This section delves into the profound impact of mentoring as a means of giving back. By sharing knowledge, experiences, and insights, we become catalysts for the growth and success of those who follow in our footsteps.

Practical guidance on becoming a mentor and fostering meaningful mentor-mentee relationships becomes a roadmap for giving back. The chapter illuminates how the act of mentoring not only benefits others but also deepens our understanding of our own journey, creating a virtuous cycle of success.

2. Contributing to the Community

Beyond individual achievements lies the expansive canvas of community contribution. This section explores the diverse ways in which we can give back to our communities—whether through philanthropy, volunteering, or other forms of contribution. Recognizing our interconnectedness and responsibility to the community enriches our lives and magnifies the impact of our success.

Real-life examples showcase the myriad ways individuals contribute to their communities, emphasizing that success is not only a personal triumph but an opportunity to create positive change in the world. The chapter underscores that a thriving community is the bedrock upon which sustained success is built.

Chapter (8) Embracing Innovation and Creativity

In the ever-evolving landscape of dreams, innovation and creativity emerge as the guiding stars that illuminate new paths and possibilities. This chapter explores the art of embracing innovation and creativity, cultivating a mindset that thrives on unconventional thinking and harnessing the power of technology to enhance productivity and realize our dreams.

A: Cultivating Creative Thinking

In the realm of dreams, creativity is the spark that ignites the fires of innovation. This section is a journey into the heart of creative thinking—a realm where ideas flourish, and imagination knows no bounds. We explore techniques for fostering creativity and breaking free from conventional thought patterns, cultivating a mindset that propels our aspirations beyond the ordinary.

1. Techniques for Fostering Creativity

Creativity is not a rare gift bestowed upon a chosen few; it's a skill that can be nurtured and expanded. This section delves into practical techniques for fostering creativity, providing a toolkit to unlock the boundless potential of innovative thinking.

- **Brainstorming:** Unleash the power of collective thinking by engaging in brainstorming sessions. This technique encourages the free flow of ideas without judgment, creating a fertile ground for creativity.

- **Mind Mapping:** Visualize connections and explore ideas through mind maps. This technique allows for nonlinear thinking, enabling the exploration of diverse pathways and relationships between concepts.

- **Lateral Thinking:** Break through mental barriers by embracing lateral thinking. This technique encourages looking at a problem from unconventional angles, fostering the discovery of novel solutions.

Practical exercises accompany each technique, guiding you to incorporate creative thinking into your daily endeavors. The chapter emphasizes that creativity is a dynamic force within everyone, waiting to be unleashed and harnessed for the realization of bold aspirations.

2. Breaking Free from Conventional Thought Patterns

Conventional thought patterns can act as chains, limiting the potential of our dreams. This section explores the importance of breaking free from traditional thinking, encouraging a mindset that challenges norms and explores uncharted territories.

- **Question Assumptions:** Interrogate assumptions underlying ideas and beliefs. By questioning the status quo, we open the door to innovative thinking and the possibility of redefining our approach to challenges.

- **Divergent Thinking:** Embrace divergent thinking, where multiple solutions are explored for a single problem. This approach fosters a mindset of abundance and possibility, encouraging the exploration of diverse perspectives.

- **Embracing Constraints:** Turn constraints into catalysts for creativity. By embracing limitations as challenges rather than obstacles, we stimulate inventive problem-solving.

Real-life examples showcase individuals who have defied conventional norms, proving that unconventional thinking can lead to transformative outcomes. The chapter guides you in cultivating a mindset that values and harnesses creativity as an essential force for progress and the realization of audacious dreams.

B: Harnessing Technology

In the digital era, technology becomes the warp and weft that weaves dreams into reality. This section is an exploration of the strategic use of technology—a powerful ally that enhances productivity and propels aspirations forward. From leveraging digital tools to adapting to the ever-evolving digital landscape, this chapter is a roadmap for harnessing technology in the pursuit of dreams.

1. Leveraging Technology to Enhance Productivity

Technology is more than a tool; it's a force multiplier that amplifies our capabilities. This section explores the ways in which we can leverage technology to enhance productivity and streamline the journey toward our aspirations.

- **Project Management Tools:**

Efficiently organize and manage tasks through project management tools. These tools provide a structured approach to goal realization, facilitating collaboration and ensuring that each step contributes to the overall progress.

- **Communication Platforms:**

Forge seamless connections and collaborations through effective communication platforms. These tools enable real-time communication, breaking down geographical barriers and fostering a dynamic exchange of ideas.

- **Automation:**

Embrace the power of automation to streamline repetitive tasks. By automating routine processes, we free up valuable time and energy for more creative and strategic endeavors.

Practical insights and recommendations accompany each strategy, guiding you in selecting and implementing technology solutions that align with your goals. The chapter underscores the importance of staying informed about technological advancements, ensuring that your toolkit remains relevant and adaptable to the evolving landscape.

2. Adapting to the Digital Landscape for Dream Realization

The digital landscape is not just a backdrop but a canvas upon which dreams can be painted with unprecedented precision. This section delves into the strategies for adapting to the digital environment to realize your aspirations.

- **Online Collaboration:**

Harness the power of online collaboration to connect with like-minded individuals and teams. The digital space offers platforms that transcend geographical boundaries, enabling collective efforts and diverse perspectives.

- **Digital Marketing:**

Navigate the digital realm to showcase your ideas and reach a global audience. Digital marketing strategies, from social media to content creation, become essential tools for amplifying your message and building a community around your aspirations.

- **Continuous Learning in the Digital Age:**

Stay abreast of advancements through online education and skill development. The digital age offers a wealth of resources for continuous learning, ensuring that you remain at the forefront of your field.

Real-world examples showcase individuals and businesses that have successfully harnessed the digital landscape to bring their dreams to fruition. The chapter provides practical guidance on navigating the digital realm, emphasizing the synergy between technological innovation and dream realization.

Chapter (9) Financial Mastery for Dream Pursuit

In the tapestry of dreams, financial mastery is the thread that weaves aspirations into tangible realities. This chapter is an exploration of the strategic elements of financial planning, encompassing budgeting for dream realization, exploring funding options, investment strategies, and fostering an entrepreneurial mindset. Join me as we delve into the realm of financial acumen to empower the pursuit of your dreams.

A: Financial Planning

In the orchestration of dream pursuit, financial planning serves as the conductor, harmonizing the intricate elements required to transform aspirations into tangible realities. This section is a journey into the art of financial planning—an essential skill that not only sustains your daily life but also propels the fulfillment of your dreams. Let's explore the nuanced aspects of budgeting for dream realization and navigating the landscape of funding options and investment strategies.

1. Budgeting for Dream Realization

Budgeting is the compass that ensures financial resources are directed purposefully toward the realization of your dreams. This exploration delves into the meticulous craft of budgeting tailored for dream pursuit. It involves:

- **Understanding Your Financial Landscape:**

Evaluate your current financial situation, considering income, expenses, and existing financial commitments. This foundational understanding provides clarity for effective financial planning.

- **Setting Realistic Financial Goals:**

Define clear and attainable financial goals aligned with your dreams. Whether it's saving for education, investing in a business, or funding a passion project, setting specific and measurable goals becomes the cornerstone of your budget.

- **Strategic Resource Allocation:**

Allocate financial resources strategically, prioritizing elements crucial for dream realization. From daily expenses to long-term investments, the budget becomes a dynamic tool that aligns your financial means with your ambitious aspirations.

Practical tips and exercises accompany this journey, empowering you to craft a budget that not only sustains your daily life but actively contributes to the funding of your dreams. The chapter emphasizes the importance of disciplined financial planning as the bedrock for the pursuit of your ultimate potential.

2. Exploring Funding Options and Investment Strategies

Dreams often require financial backing to transform from vision to reality. This section embarks on an exploration of funding options and investment strategies, ensuring that financial decisions align with the nature and timelines of your aspirations. It involves:

- **Traditional Avenues:**

Explore conventional funding sources such as savings, loans, and personal investments. Understand the advantages and limitations of each, tailoring your approach to match the unique financial requirements of your dreams.

- **Modern Approaches:**

Embrace contemporary funding methods like crowdfunding, angel investors, and investment portfolios. This exploration provides insights into diversification, risk management, and long-term financial planning.

Insights into the dynamic landscape of financial instruments guide you in making informed decisions about funding your dreams. The chapter underscores the importance of aligning your financial strategies with the distinct characteristics of your aspirations, ensuring a symbiotic relationship between your dreams and your financial journey.

B: Entrepreneurial Mindset

In the symphony of dream pursuit, the entrepreneurial mindset is the melody that harmonizes passion, innovation, and strategic thinking. This section is an exploration into fostering an entrepreneurial mindset—a transformative approach that enables the building of businesses around your passions and navigating the challenges inherent in entrepreneurship.

1. Building a Business Around Your Passion

For those with an entrepreneurial spirit, turning a passion into a thriving business is a profound journey. This exploration delves into the foundational elements of entrepreneurship, guiding you through the process of:

- **Identifying Your Passion:**

Uncover the core passions that fuel your aspirations. This introspective journey lays the groundwork for aligning your business endeavors with your personal dreams.

- **Market Research:**

Understand the landscape in which your business will operate. Conduct thorough market research to identify opportunities, challenges, and potential niches for your passion-driven enterprise.

- **Business Planning:**

Craft a robust business plan that outlines your vision, mission, target audience, and revenue streams. A well-structured plan becomes the roadmap for transforming your passion into a sustainable and thriving business.

- **Execution:**

Take intentional steps to bring your business to life. From branding to marketing and operations, the execution phase is where your passion transforms into a tangible and marketable offering.

Real-world examples and practical guidance accompany each stage, empowering you to navigate the intricate path of building a business around your passion. The chapter emphasizes that an entrepreneurial mindset is not just about profit but about creating a venture that resonates with your personal aspirations.

2. Navigating the Challenges of Entrepreneurship

The entrepreneurial path is marked by challenges and opportunities for growth. This section addresses the common obstacles faced by entrepreneurs and provides strategies for navigating them. It involves:

- **Financial Risks:**

Manage financial risks by understanding the financial landscape of your business. From budgeting to investment decisions, a proactive approach to financial management becomes a shield against potential challenges.

- **Resilience:**

Cultivate resilience in the face of setbacks. Entrepreneurship is a journey filled with highs and lows; developing the ability to bounce back from challenges is essential for long-term success.

- **Strategic Thinking:**

Foster strategic thinking by continually evaluating and adapting your business strategies. Embrace a mindset that views challenges as opportunities for innovation and growth.

Insights from seasoned entrepreneurs, case studies, and practical advice form a comprehensive guide for navigating the challenges of entrepreneurship. The chapter underscores that an entrepreneurial mindset is not just about building a business but about cultivating a mindset that thrives in the pursuit of ambitious dreams.

Chapter (10) Navigating Personal and Professional Relationships

In the intricate dance of dream pursuit, the relationships we foster—both personal and professional—shape the rhythm of our journey. This chapter is a guide to navigating the delicate balance between personal and professional connections. We'll explore strategies for maintaining harmony, handling conflicts and stress, as well as honing effective networking skills to leverage social connections for opportunities.

A: Balancing Relationships

In the mosaic of dream pursuit, the delicate balance between personal and professional relationships is an art that, when mastered, adds richness and depth to the journey. This chapter is a guide to navigating the intricate dance of maintaining harmony between personal and professional life. We'll explore strategies for setting boundaries, effective time management, and fostering open communication to ensure that your pursuit of dreams enhances, rather than hinders, your relationships.

1. Maintaining Harmony Between Personal and Professional Life

Setting Boundaries

The canvas of your life is divided into personal and professional realms, each deserving its own space and attention. This section explores the importance of setting boundaries:

Defining Clear Boundaries: Clearly delineate the boundaries between personal and professional life. Establishing these limits helps create a structured environment that allows for dedicated focus on both aspects without undue interference.

- **Preserving Personal Time:** Allocate specific time for personal relationships, ensuring that your loved ones receive the attention and presence they deserve. This intentional approach strengthens the bonds that sustain you on your journey.

- **Preserving Professional Focus:** Similarly, carve out focused time for your professional endeavors. By immersing yourself in work during designated periods, you enhance productivity and prevent it from encroaching on your personal life.

Effective Time Management

Balancing relationships requires a skillful mastery of time. This section delves into effective time management:

- **Prioritizing Responsibilities:** Identify and prioritize responsibilities in both personal and professional spheres. By understanding the critical tasks in each area, you can allocate time effectively and prevent one from overwhelming the other.

- **Creating a Balanced Schedule:** Craft a well-organized schedule that accommodates both personal and professional commitments. A balanced schedule allows for the pursuit of dreams without neglecting the essential connections that anchor your life.

- **Adaptability in Time Allocation:** Recognize that priorities may shift over time. Stay adaptable and be willing to adjust your time allocation to accommodate changing circumstances and evolving aspirations.

Open Communication

Communication is the bridge that connects personal and professional worlds. This section emphasizes the importance of open and transparent communication:

- **Sharing Aspirations:** Communicate your dreams and aspirations openly with your loved ones and colleagues. Sharing your goals fosters understanding and invites support, creating a collaborative atmosphere that propels your journey forward.

- **Expressing Needs:** Articulate your needs and expectations in both personal and professional relationships. Honest communication allows for mutual understanding, preventing misunderstandings that can strain connections.

- **Active Listening:** Cultivate the art of active listening. By attentively listening to the needs and aspirations of others, you strengthen your connections and build relationships based on empathy and understanding.

Real-world scenarios and practical exercises accompany each strategy, providing you with actionable steps to navigate the delicate balance between personal and professional relationships. As you embark on this exploration, celebrate the richness that meaningful connections bring to your journey.

B: Networking for Success

In the expansive tapestry of dream pursuit, networking becomes the loom that weaves together opportunities, collaborations, and shared aspirations. This section is a guide to honing effective networking skills and leveraging social connections to propel your dreams forward.

1. Effective Networking Skills

Authentic Relationship Building

Networking is more than transactions; it's the art of building meaningful and authentic connections. This section explores effective networking skills:

- **Genuine Engagement:** Foster authentic connections by genuinely engaging with others. Instead of approaching networking as a transactional exchange, focus on building relationships based on mutual respect and shared values.

- **Active Listening and Communication**: Hone active listening and communication skills. By truly understanding the needs and aspirations of others, you position yourself as a valuable collaborator within your network.

- **Strategic Relationship Building:** Develop a strategic approach to networking by identifying key individuals and communities relevant to your goals. Intentional networking opens doors to opportunities and collaborations that can accelerate the realization of your dreams.

2. Leveraging Social Connections for Opportunities

Building a Diverse Network

A robust network is a diverse network. This section guides you in cultivating a network that spans industries, professions, and interests:

- **Diversity in Perspectives:** A diverse network provides a wealth of perspectives and insights. Embrace connections with individuals who bring different experiences and backgrounds to the table, enriching your understanding and expanding your horizons.

- **Collaborative Opportunities:** Cultivate a collaborative environment within your network. By offering support and expertise to others, you create a reciprocal atmosphere where opportunities flow organically.

- **Strategic Visibility:** Strategically position yourself within your network to enhance visibility. Actively contribute to discussions, share your expertise, and participate in relevant events to increase your presence and open doors to new possibilities.

Real-world examples and practical guidance accompany each stage of effective networking, empowering you to build a network that goes beyond the superficial and becomes a dynamic force in your journey.

Chapter (11) Environmental Consciousness and Social Impact

In the mosaic of dream pursuit, the impact we make on the world becomes a defining brushstroke. This chapter is a guide to aligning dreams with social responsibility, exploring the incorporation of sustainability into personal goals, making a positive impact on communities and the environment, and delving into the realm of social entrepreneurship. Join me in this exploration of dreams that not only fulfill personal aspirations but also contribute to the betterment of the world.

A: Aligning Dreams with Social Responsibility

In the journey of pursuing our dreams, the impact we have on the world becomes a profound expression of our values and aspirations. This chapter is a guide to aligning dreams with social responsibility, exploring ways to incorporate sustainability into personal goals and make a positive impact on communities and the environment.

1. Incorporating Sustainability into Personal Goals
Environmental Consciousness

Dreams that reflect environmental consciousness contribute to a sustainable future. This section encourages you to:

- **Evaluate Ecological Footprint:** Consider the environmental impact of your goals. Explore ways to minimize resource consumption, reduce waste, and make environmentally conscious choices in your pursuit of dreams.

- **Ethical Decision-Making:** Infuse ethical considerations into your decision-making process. Strive to align your goals with sustainable practices, ensuring that your journey is characterized by responsibility and respect for the planet.

- **Global Impact:** Acknowledge the global ramifications of your dreams. Explore how your aspirations can be harnessed to contribute positively to broader sustainability initiatives, fostering a sense of global responsibility.

2. Making a Positive Impact on Communities and the Environment

Community Engagement

Dreams that uplift communities and the environment create lasting legacies. This section provides strategies for making a positive impact:

- **Community-Centric Approach:** Engage actively with local communities impacted by your dreams. Listen to their needs, understand their concerns, and collaborate on initiatives that contribute positively to the social fabric.

- **Philanthropy and Giving Back:** Integrate philanthropy into your dreams. Consider how your success can be channeled back into the communities that support your journey. Whether through charitable initiatives or community development projects, giving back becomes an integral part of your dream pursuit.

- **Educational Initiatives:** Utilize your dreams as a platform for education. Raise awareness about social and environmental issues, leveraging your influence to inspire positive change and empower others to contribute to a better world.

B: Social Entrepreneurship

In the realm of dream pursuit, social entrepreneurship emerges as a dynamic force that not only realizes business goals but also creates meaningful and positive societal impact. This chapter is a guide to understanding the principles of social entrepreneurship, merging business goals with a commitment to social change, and exploring case studies of successful social entrepreneurs who have navigated this transformative path.

1. Merging Business Goals with Social Impact
Purpose-Driven Business

Social entrepreneurship is characterized by a purpose-driven approach that seeks to bring about positive change. This section explores the principles of merging business goals with social impact:

- **Infusing Purpose:** Embed purpose into your business goals. Consider how your enterprise can address social or environmental challenges, making a tangible contribution to the betterment of society.

- **Measuring Impact:** Develop metrics to measure the social impact of your business. From job creation to environmental sustainability, quantifying the positive outcomes ensures that your business goals align with meaningful change.

- **Collaborative Partnerships:** Forge partnerships with organizations and initiatives that share your social impact goals. Collaborative efforts amplify the reach and effectiveness of your business in creating positive change.

2. Case Studies of Successful Social Entrepreneurs
Inspiring Examples

Real-world examples illuminate the path to successful social entrepreneurship. This section showcases case studies of individuals who have effectively merged business goals with social impact:

- **The Grameen Bank :** The Grameen Bank pioneered

microfinance, providing small loans to empower individuals in poverty, particularly women, to start their own businesses. This approach not only lifted people out of poverty but also fostered economic independence.

- **TOMS Shoes** : TOMS Shoes operates on a "One for One" model, donating a pair of shoes for every pair sold. By addressing a basic need in impoverished communities, TOMS has become a symbol of conscious consumerism and philanthropy.

- **Patagonia** : Patagonia is a leader in sustainable and ethical business practices. The company actively advocates for environmental causes and responsible consumption, demonstrating that profitability and environmental responsibility can coexist.

Chapter (12) Mastery of Self-Discovery

In the intricate journey of pursuing dreams, the mastery of self-discovery becomes the compass that guides us towards authentic living and fulfillment. This chapter is a guide to exploring personal values, identifying core beliefs, and aligning goals with authenticity. Additionally, we will delve into practices for mindfulness and emotional resilience, and explore the integration of spirituality into the pursuit of dreams.

A: Exploring Personal Values

In the mosaic of self-discovery, exploring personal values becomes the palette that shapes the authentic hues of our aspirations. This chapter is a guide to identifying core values for authentic living, understanding the principles and beliefs that define your essence, and aligning your goals with a foundation of authenticity.

1. Identifying Core Values for Authentic Living

Self-Reflection

Embarking on the journey of self-discovery involves a deliberate and introspective exploration of your core values. This section encourages you to:

- **Reflect on Beliefs:** Take time to reflect on the principles and beliefs that resonate deeply with your identity. What values define your character and guide your decision-making?

- **Clarify Priorities:** Identify the values that are non-negotiable in your life. These may include principles such as integrity, compassion, creativity, or any other virtues that hold significant meaning for you.

- **Evaluate Alignment:** Consider how your current life aligns with these identified values. Are your actions, goals, and relationships in harmony with your core beliefs, or are there areas that require realignment?

2. Aligning Goals with Personal Beliefs
Harmony of Aspirations

A profound sense of fulfillment arises when your goals align with your personal beliefs. This section guides you in creating a synergy between your aspirations and your authentic self:

- **Evaluate Goal Alignment:** Assess each of your goals against your identified core values. Do they reflect and uphold the principles that matter most to you?

- **Adjusting Aspirations:** If there are inconsistencies between your goals and values, consider how you might adjust your aspirations. This doesn't necessarily mean compromising your dreams but rather refining them to be in harmony with your authentic self.

- **Holistic Perspective:** Adopt a holistic perspective that considers not only the external achievements but also the internal satisfaction that comes from living in alignment with your values.

B: Spiritual and Emotional Well-being

In the intricate tapestry of self-discovery, the threads of spiritual and emotional well-being weave a resilient and harmonious fabric. This chapter is a guide to practices that enhance mindfulness, foster emotional resilience, and explore the integration of spirituality into the pursuit of dreams.

1. Practices for Mindfulness and Emotional Resilience
Mindfulness Techniques

Mindfulness is the art of being present, a cornerstone of emotional resilience. This section explores practical techniques to enhance mindfulness:

- **Meditation Practices:** Cultivate a meditation routine to quiet the mind, enhance self-awareness, and develop a sense of inner calm.

- **Mindful Breathing:** Incorporate mindful breathing exercises into your daily life. Conscious and intentional breathing is a powerful tool for grounding yourself in the present moment.

- **Mindful Observation:** Practice mindful observation of your thoughts and emotions without judgment. This awareness allows you to respond to situations with clarity and composure.

Emotional Resilience
Emotional resilience is the capacity to bounce back from challenges. This section provides strategies to build emotional strength:

- **Acceptance of Emotions:** Acknowledge and accept your emotions without judgment. Embracing your feelings allows for a healthier processing of challenges.

- **Positive Coping Mechanisms:** Develop positive coping mechanisms for stress and adversity. Whether through exercise, creative outlets, or social support, having effective coping strategies is crucial for emotional resilience.

- **Learn from Setbacks:** View setbacks as opportunities for growth. Extracting lessons from challenges enables you to navigate future obstacles with greater wisdom.

2. Integrating Spirituality into the Pursuit of Dreams
Connecting with Purpose

Spirituality adds depth and purpose to the pursuit of dreams. This section explores ways to integrate spirituality into your journey:

- **Reflecting on Purpose:** Contemplate the spiritual dimensions of your goals. Consider how your aspirations contribute to a higher purpose or serve the greater good.

- **Practical Spiritual Practices:** Incorporate practical spiritual practices into your routine. These can include prayer, meditation, or rituals that provide moments of reflection and connection.

- **Holistic Fulfillment:** Recognize that spiritual fulfillment contributes to a holistic sense of well-being. By aligning your goals with a deeper purpose, you infuse your journey with meaning beyond external achievements.

Chapter (13) Global Perspectives on Dream Fulfillment

In the interconnected world we inhabit, understanding and navigating diverse cultural landscapes is pivotal to the pursuit of dreams. This chapter is a guide to exploring cultural influences on dreams, understanding diverse perspectives on success, learning from global success stories, and breaking barriers that may arise due to cultural, geographical, and societal limitations. Additionally, we will delve into fostering a global mindset for the achievement of dreams.

A: Cultural Influences on Dreams

In the kaleidoscope of human experience, cultural influences play a profound role in shaping our dreams and perceptions of success. This chapter is a guide to understanding diverse cultural perspectives on success, learning from global success stories, and appreciating the impact of cultural backgrounds on our pursuit of dreams.

1. Understanding Diverse Cultural Perspectives on Success
Cultural Self-Reflection

Our cultural backgrounds shape the lens through which we view success. This section encourages you to embark on a journey of cultural self-reflection:

- **Reflect on Cultural Values:** Consider the cultural values embedded in your upbringing. How have these values influenced your definition of success, and what role do they play in your dreams?

- **Questioning Assumptions:** Challenge assumptions about success rooted in your cultural background. Explore whether these assumptions align with your authentic aspirations or if they are shaped by external expectations.

- **Embracing Cultural Pluralism**: Embrace the idea that success is culturally plural. Recognize that diverse cultures celebrate a variety of accomplishments, ranging from individual achievements to contributions to the community.

2. Learning from Global Success Stories
Cultural Case Studies

The world is a tapestry woven with success stories from various cultural threads. This section invites you to explore and learn from global success stories:

- **Diverse Definitions of Success:** Study success stories from different cultures and regions. Understand how success is defined in these contexts, and appreciate the diversity of paths individuals take to achieve their dreams.

- **Cultural Nuances in Leadership:** Examine leadership styles in various cultural settings. Recognize how cultural nuances influence leadership approaches, communication styles, and the attainment of goals.

- **Incorporating Cultural Wisdom:** Extract wisdom from diverse cultural approaches to problem-solving and decision-making. Incorporate these insights into your own journey, fostering adaptability and a broader perspective.

B: Breaking Barriers

In the pursuit of dreams, barriers may manifest due to cultural, geographical, and societal limitations. This chapter serves as a guide to overcoming these barriers, fostering a global mindset, and embracing the richness that comes from navigating diverse environments.

1. Overcoming Cultural, Geographical, and Societal Limitations
Cultural Sensitivity
Cultural, geographical, and societal limitations can present unique challenges. This section provides strategies for overcoming these barriers:

- **Cultural Sensitivity:** Develop cultural sensitivity as a tool for breaking down barriers. Understand and appreciate cultural nuances to foster meaningful connections with individuals from diverse backgrounds.

- **Adaptability:** Cultivate adaptability to navigate different cultural environments. Recognize that flexibility in communication styles, business practices, and social norms is key to overcoming cultural limitations.

- **Respect for Diversity:** Embrace the diversity of cultural perspectives. Celebrate differences rather than seeing them as obstacles, and leverage the strengths that emerge from a multicultural approach to problem-solving.

2. Fostering a Global Mindset for Dream Achievement
Embracing Global Perspectives
A global mindset is a powerful asset in breaking down barriers and expanding the horizons of dream achievement. This section guides you in cultivating a global perspective:

- **Cultural Intelligence:** Develop cultural intelligence to navigate diverse environments effectively. This involves understanding and adapting to different cultural norms, communication styles, and business practices.

- **Language Skills:** Acquire language skills that facilitate global communication. The ability to communicate in different languages opens doors to broader connections and opportunities.

- **Continuous Learning:** Cultivate a mindset of continuous learning about global trends, perspectives, and opportunities. This proactive approach enables you to adapt and thrive in an ever-evolving global landscape.

❖ Conclusion

In the final chapter of our journey, we take a moment to reflect on the key points explored throughout this blueprint for achieving your ultimate potential. This chapter provides a concise recap of the essential elements discussed and offers words of encouragement and inspiration to empower you on your path to dream fulfillment.

A: Recap of Key Points

In this concluding chapter, let's revisit the fundamental elements that form the backbone of your journey toward realizing your ultimate potential.

1. Definition of Dreams

a. Personal Aspirations and Goals:

Dreams encapsulate your deepest aspirations and goals, representing the authentic desires that propel you forward.

b. Importance of Pursuing Dreams:

Pursuing dreams transcends the personal realm, influencing not only your life but also contributing to the positive transformation of the world.

2. The Power of Dreams

a. Motivational Stories:

Real-life narratives of individuals who transformed their dreams into reality serve as potent sources of inspiration, underscoring the transformative influence of unwavering commitment.

b. Scientific and Psychological Perspectives:

Understanding the scientific and psychological dimensions of dreams reinforces their impact on motivation, resilience, and overall well-being.

B. Encouragement and Inspiration for Readers

a. Embracing the Journey:

- **Resilience:** Embrace challenges as opportunities for growth, recognizing that resilience is key to overcoming setbacks.

- **Adaptability:** Be flexible and open to change, learning from every experience that shapes your journey.
- **Courage:** Approach your aspirations boldly, facing challenges with determination and unwavering courage.

b. Acknowledging Achievements:

- **Reflection:** Take moments to reflect on your progress, acknowledging and celebrating the milestones achieved along the way.
- **Learning from Setbacks:** View setbacks as stepping stones for growth, extracting valuable lessons to refine your approach.

c. Sustaining Success:

- **Balancing Work and Life:** Prioritize self-care and maintain a healthy work-life balance to avoid burnout.
- **Giving Back:** Consider contributing to others and your community as you achieve success, fostering a sense of purpose beyond personal goals.

Final Words

Your journey is a unique tapestry, woven with the threads of your aspirations, resilience, and growth. As you move forward, remember that the power to define and pursue your dreams authentically resides within you. Embrace the process, learn from every experience, and believe in the limitless potential that lies within.

.B: Encouragement and Inspiration for Readers

In this concluding chapter, let's draw inspiration and encouragement from the insights shared on the journey towards realizing your ultimate potential.

Embracing the Journey

1. Resilience:

- **Message:** Embrace challenges as opportunities for growth.
- **Reflection:** In moments of adversity, recognize that resilience is the key to not only overcoming setbacks but emerging stronger.

2. Adaptability:

- **Message:** Be flexible and open to change.
- **Reflection:** The ability to adapt to evolving circumstances and learn from experiences is a crucial aspect of navigating your journey.

3. Courage:

- **Message:** Approach your aspirations boldly.
- **Reflection:** Facing challenges with determination and unwavering courage propels you closer to the realization of your dreams.

Acknowledging Achievements
1. Reflection:

- **Message:** Take time to reflect on your progress.
- **Reflection:** Regular moments of reflection allow you to acknowledge and celebrate the milestones achieved along your unique path.

2. Learning from Setbacks:

- **Message:** View setbacks as stepping stones for growth.
- **Reflection:** Extract valuable lessons from setbacks, recognizing them as opportunities to refine your approach and build resilience.

Sustaining Success
1. Balancing Work and Life:

- **Message:** Prioritize self-care and maintain a healthy work-life balance.
- **Reflection:** Avoid burnout by ensuring that self-care is an integral part of your journey, allowing you to sustain success over the long term.

2. Giving Back:

- **Message:** Consider contributing to others and your community.
- **Reflection:** As you achieve success, find fulfillment in giving back, fostering a sense of purpose that extends beyond personal goals.

Final Words

Your journey is a dynamic, evolving narrative shaped by your dreams, resilience, and continuous growth. As you move forward, remember that the power to define and pursue your dreams authentically resides within you.

May your path be illuminated with moments of fulfillment, purpose, and the unwavering courage to dream beyond boundaries. Your potential knows no bounds, and the world eagerly awaits the unique contributions only you can make.

Onward to the next chapter of your extraordinary journey!